ESCAPE

Escape

Richard A. Boning

Illustrated by

Jim Sharpe

The Incredible Series

Barnell Loft, Ltd. Baldwin, New York

To
Eva B. Lofty

"I can do it," A.B. Jones said hopefully. "I can escape." William Craft felt a twinge of pity as he glanced at his friend's pipestem arms and legs. Not even the strongest, cleverest slave had ever escaped from the area of Macon, Georgia.

That night William listened carefully as he lay in his crude cabin. No sound of dogs yet! Maybe A.B. would succeed. Then William's heart turned to stone as the baying of hounds rang through the night. Next there was frantic barking. He shivered. For a long time he lay awake thinking of what would happen to his friend tomorrow.

The next morning, December 21, 1848, William trudged to Macon. Every slave in the area was required to be in the town square to witness the punishment. This included his wife, Ellen, who belonged to another owner. All the slaves spoke in fearful whispers. They knew the punishment would be severe.

Crack! In the hand of the whipmaster, the lash seemed alive. It left a bright red ribbon across the back of A.B. Jones. Time after time the lash whistled and drew blood. A.B. began to slump; his eyes closed, and William felt fear clutch at his heart. He wanted to cry out, but didn't dare. The slave catchers, Hughes and Knight, were watching him closely.

Hughes spoke. "You're a bright kind of nigger. You learned cabinetmaking better than any one." He paused, and his pale, gray, almost colorless eyes grew cold. "Just be sure, Craft, that you don't get *too* bright."

William choked down his anger. He knew that Hughes was taunting him. The slave catcher wanted him to try to escape. He was daring him to make the next bid for freedom. And the incredible thing about it was that this was exactly what William intended to do! For four long years he and Ellen had talked about it, but they had not yet thought of a good plan.

Suddenly the whipmaster grunted. "He's dead." Hughes sauntered slowly over to the whipping post. Indifferently he placed the toe of his boot against A.B.'s back. He shoved. Slowly the body slid down the post, lifeless. "Too much lash," said Hughes, matter-of-factly. "No problem though. It was a corrective accident."

Rage surged through William's body. Under the laws of the State of Georgia, a slave could be killed while being "corrected." For a moment he wanted to spring at the slave catcher. But his wife placed her hand in his and squeezed gently. His self-control returned.

As the slaves returned to their quarters, William whispered to Ellen, "We're going to escape. I've got an idea that will take some nerve, but I think it will work."

"I'm afraid," she said simply. "So afraid I don't know what to do."

She glanced over her shoulder. Behind them walked Hughes. On his face was a knowing look.

13

Escape had been on William's mind for a long time. When he was fourteen years old, he had been sold away from his parents. His thirteen-year-old sister had been sold also. As her new owner had placed her in his wagon, William had stared from the auction block. His sister was sobbing. He never saw her again.

Ellen stared at him with disbelief.

Grinning, he explained. "While the slave catchers are looking in the woods and swamps, we'll be on a train. We'll go in style and live in the finest hotels!"

Ellen looked at him, open-mouthed.

"It sounds crazy," he agreed. "But it can work. We've got the money." His master had often hired him out to other plantation owners, and he was allowed to keep a small part of his earnings.

Ellen stared at him. "But how — how — ?"

"You will go as the master," William said. His excitement grew. "I will be your slave." As he spoke, he stared at Ellen's light skin. Then she understood. She was often mistaken for a white person.

But it was insane. It numbed her just to think about it. "Oh no!" she gasped. "We could never get away with it."

Without even hearing her, William began to open the bag he had brought with him. Taking out a silk hat, he continued. "You will dress like a man. Your eyes are too pretty for a man's so we'll cover them with green glasses. You mustn't talk much."

The thought of the danger was too much for Ellen. "But how will I sign the hotel register? I can't read or write."

William had thought of this too. "Your arm will be in a sling," he explained. "You won't be able to use it. Ellen, you are going to be very ill. I will take you north to Philadelphia to be cured."

Ellen looked at him doubtfully. "It's 1,000 miles to Philadelphia," she said in hushed tones. "Any white person who found out could claim us. Then there are the slave catchers." At the thought of Hughes and Knight, she shuddered. "They'll come after us," she predicted.

"They can't catch us if we get a good head start," said William. "And besides, they won't know where to look."

Both of them knew that she would have to do an incredible job of acting and have nerves of steel. "We can try," she said. It was clear she was not convinced.

Four days later Ellen found herself before the ticket window at the train station in Macon. She fully expected the ticket agent to recognize her. He would laugh scornfully. Then he would promptly turn the two of them over to the slave catchers. She braced herself. Instead she was amazed to find him polite and respectful. "Tickets for you and your slave, sir?" he asked.

Barely able to speak, she gulped and answered, "Yes — to Philadelphia." William escorted her to a car for white passengers only. Before going back to the slave car, he told her softly, "Keep your nerve. Don't talk unless you have to."

Ellen nodded numbly. With her heart hammering, she boarded the train. Without William she felt even more nervous. The car was filled with planters and merchants. She found an empty seat by a window. Hopefully, no one would sit beside her. Then she saw a sight that made her gasp in disbelief.

Hughes and Knight were boarding the train! It was just like the nightmare she had had for the past four nights. Hughes was holding a shotgun. A pistol was strapped to Knight's hip. How had the slave catchers known of their escape? Not daring to breathe, Ellen watched, as Hughes whispered to the conductor.

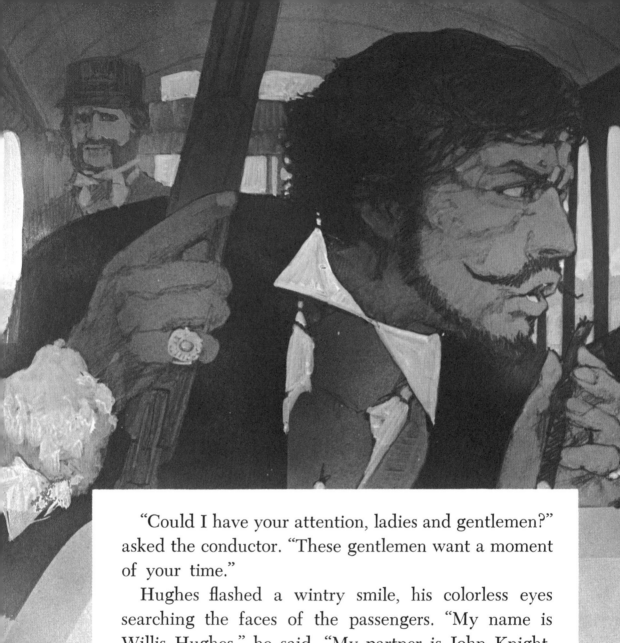

"Could I have your attention, ladies and gentlemen?" asked the conductor. "These gentlemen want a moment of your time."

Hughes flashed a wintry smile, his colorless eyes searching the faces of the passengers. "My name is Willis Hughes," he said. "My partner is John Knight. We have information that five runaway slaves have been seen in the Eatonton area. We're going to ride up there and look for them. If you're getting off at that stop and see anything suspicious, please get in touch with us. Just leave word at the Eatonton Hotel."

Ellen dared to breathe again. They were looking for someone else! But her joy was short-lived. Striding down the aisle came Hughes and Knight. Hughes, by-passing a dozen empty seats, sat down beside *her!* She quickly turned her head toward the window. In the reflection she could see Hughes studying her. At any moment she expected a strong hand to grab her by the shoulder.

Then came the very words that she had heard in her nightmare! "Haven't I seen you somewhere before, sir?" Hughes asked.

Ellen couldn't believe it. The train had barely left the station and they were about to be captured. She did not trust herself to answer.

Raising his voice, now edged with suspicion, Hughes repeated the question. Other passengers snickered at his annoyance, and he flushed angrily. But Ellen was too terrified to speak.

"No need to be harsh, Mr. Hughes," said a nearby passenger. "The young gentleman is obviously deaf."

Now almost shouting, Hughes tried once again. "Sir, I have the feeling we have met before. Have we?"

Should she speak? Would her voice betray her? If she didn't answer, his suspicions would be confirmed. She had no choice. Mustering all her courage, Ellen finally turned toward him. "No," she said, her voice tight with fear.

Hughes grunted, not convinced. After the train had stopped at Eatonton and began to pull away, Ellen glanced back. To her dismay, the slave catchers were on the platform. They were staring at her. As the train gathered speed, a look of recognition dawned on Hughes' face. He began to talk excitedly with Knight. Then both of them were running after the train. It was too late — for the moment. But Ellen knew that she and William had lost the head start they needed so desperately.

That night when they got off the train in Charleston, Ellen was weary from the strain. As they crossed the lobby of the hotel, she felt every pair of eyes in the room on them. The pressure was beginning to tell. Dizziness swept over her. Then she felt William's strong hand on her elbow. "Be careful now, young master," he said. "Don't exert yourself." Gently he guided her across the lobby. A murmur of approval arose from the onlookers. "That's a mighty fine nigger," said one of them.

29

To the hotel manager William explained that Ellen could not sign the register. "It's young master's arm," he said sorrowfully. "He hurt it riding to hounds." There was sympathy among the bystanders — and agreement. "He's got the look of a horseman", said one man. "A Tidewater aristocrat," murmured a woman.

The hotel manager nodded and led them to a fine room. "Your master can have one of our best rooms. If he is not up to eating in the dining room, I shall tell the cook, and you can bring up his supper for him."

When the door was shut, they both breathed a sigh of relief. William smiled slightly. "Master, you should stop riding to hounds," he said. But Ellen's smile was faint.

In the kitchen William received a shock. The cook, a large and merry black man, was polite and agreeable, and he had the most knowing eyes that William had ever seen. He looked like a man who was capable of anything.

"Pompey fix two plate," the cook said in musical tones. "You eat with young master?" he asked. Then he paused and looked around. Satisfied that no one was listening, he smiled and said, "You both need strength if you escape to North."

William was stunned. "But how — how could you possibly know?"

Pompey chuckled. "When I see you help young master, I know *not* white. Pompey know what he know." He raised his eyebrows in amusement.

Could William trust this man? There was no choice. Pompey already knew their secret.

Pompey flashed a huge smile. "Pompey be ready to welcome visitors," he said, glancing at a box under the table. William stared into it, but it only contained unlabeled bottles. One of them was filled with a dark brown liquid.

Nervously William thanked him. Perhaps he should not have told him anything. As William left with Ellen's dinner, a vicious-looking white man entered the kitchen. The man turned abruptly and began to speak to Pompey in low tones. With a start, William realized that they must be friends. Was Pompey about to betray them?

Late that night a carriage pulled up to the front of the Calhoun Hotel. Two familiar figures got out. "They've got to be here," said Hughes. "The driver told me he let them off tonight."

Knight's lips parted in a smile. "Looks like we'll be having another public meeting in the town square back in Macon," he said.

Hughes approached the clerk at the desk and asked a few questions. "They're here," he told Knight. "I've even got the room number. The man's out in the slave quarters somewhere."

"Let's not stir up things until we know where he is," said Knight. "Let's ask the cook if he knows."

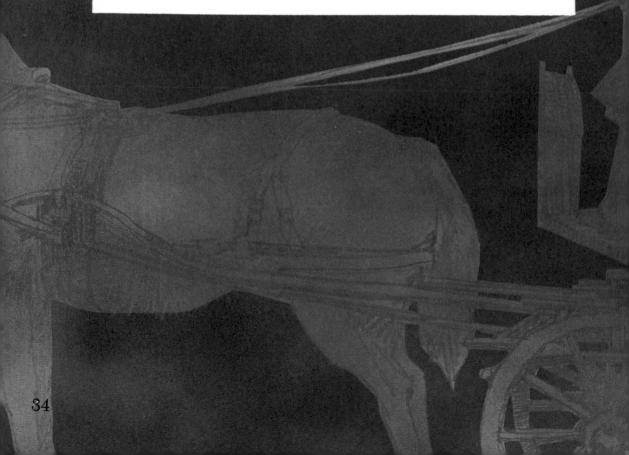

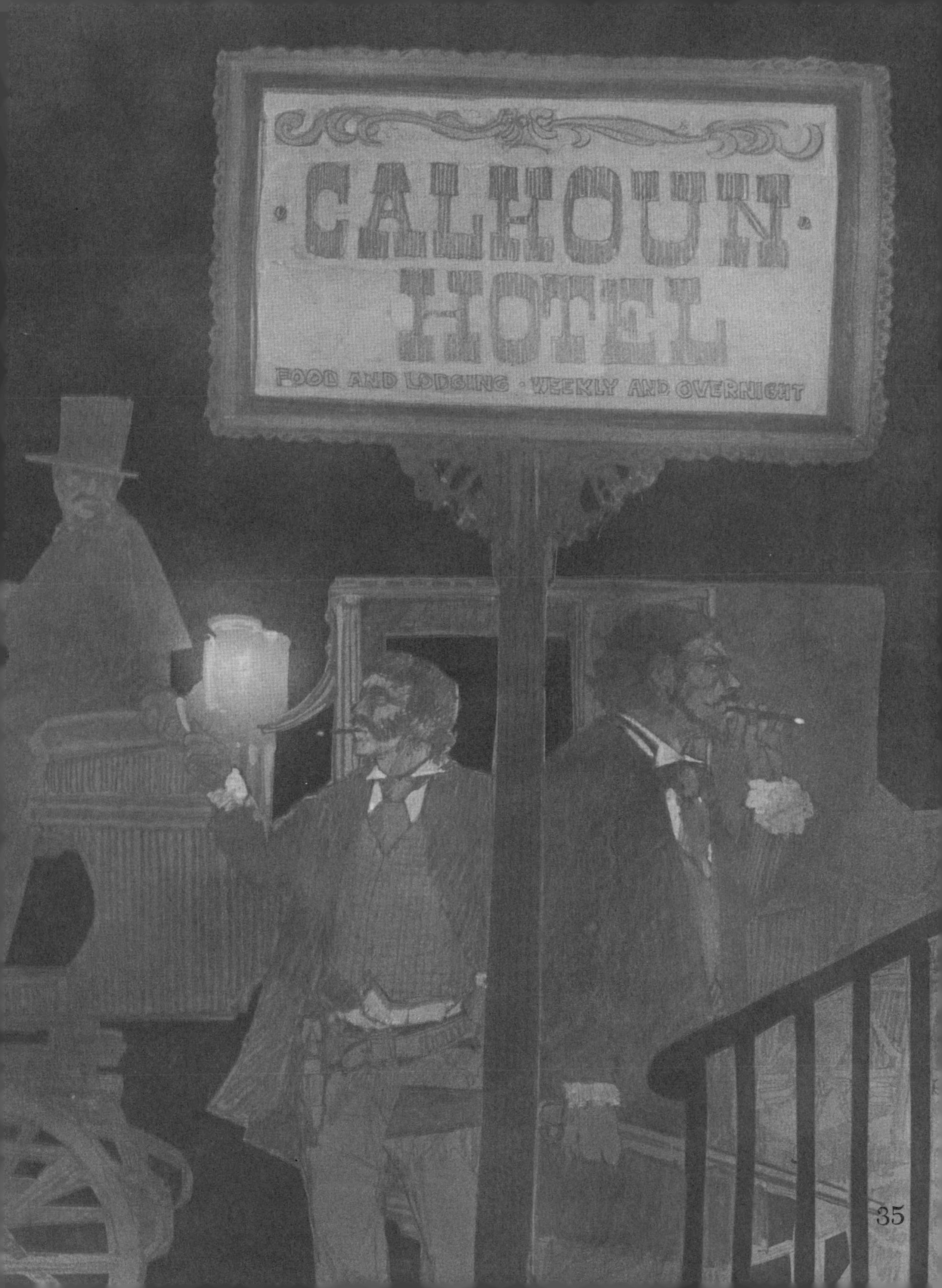
CALHOUN HOTEL
FOOD AND LODGING · WEEKLY AND OVERNIGHT

In the kitchen Pompey appeared confused. "You say white man and black woman?"

"No, you blasted fool!" snarled Hughes, "a white woman — I mean a woman who looks white — and a black man."

"Why white woman travel with black man?" asked Pompey.

Hughes swore explosively, but Pompey maintained a look of childlike innocence.

"Forget it," said Knight. "All he's good for is cooking." He had an idea. "Say, we know where the runaways are. They're not going anywhere tonight. Let's eat first."

"Don't be a fool," said Hughes. "We've already spent all day on the road."

"That's just it. Those slaves aren't going anywhere, and I'm hungry," said Knight.

Pompey brought some chicken from the oven. "Taste fine, masters." He laughed. "Like no meat you ever have. Pompey fix plate for you."

Grudgingly, Hughes nodded.

The chicken was delicious. But as they ate, the room started to spin.

"Don't worry, master," said Pompey. "Pompey take good care of you." Both men tried to get up, but they fell to the floor, unconscious. The last thing they heard was the sound of Pompey's mocking laughter.

The next morning William looked out of his cabin behind the hotel. He saw something that made him rub his eyes. Hughes and Knight were bound in a line of blacks being herded down the road! Only it wasn't Hughes and Knight. Or was it? Their skins were black! Behind them was the white man that William had seen talking to Pompey. Evidently he was taking a shipment of slaves to be sold.

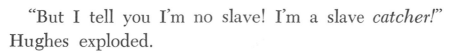

"But I tell you I'm no slave! I'm a slave *catcher!*"
Hughes exploded.

"Shut up. I told you I wasn't going to give you another warning."

Quickly William made his way to the kitchen. What had happened? Were he and Ellen destined to be part of that same shipment of slaves? Had Pompey somehow coated Hughes and Knight with Trader's Tan?

"Maybe so," Pompey agreed. He smiled and proudly displayed a stack of coins. "Man give me nice money for two new slaves. Maybe real soon I go to freedom too." His laughter boomed, rich and mellow. Quickly he became serious. "Careful in Baltimore," he warned. "Baltimore be more bad than Hughes and Knight. Baltimore catch more slaves than those two ever see." He turned away and began preparing food. As William left, he could still hear Pompey chuckling softly to himself.

For the next four days Ellen continued to hold up bravely under the strain. But her strength was going. With relief the two finally arrived in Baltimore.

As they waited for their tickets, two men pulled a kicking, thrashing black man away from the ticket window. "But I am a freedman!" he kept shouting. Deaf to all his pleas, they dragged him away. "That's what they all say," chuckled a bystander. "But they find that Baltimore's a pretty tough nut to crack — even when some fool has given them their freedom."

At this, William's blood ran cold. If a freedman could be hauled back into slavery, what chance did he and Ellen have? He did not have to wait long to find out.

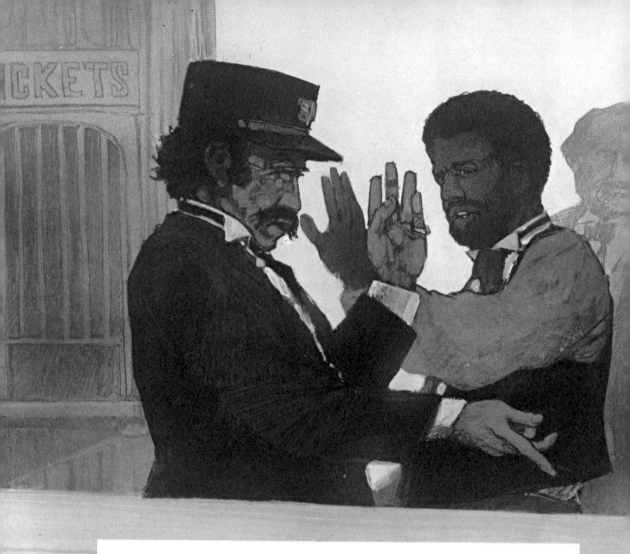

"You got papers for that slave?" the ticket agent asked Ellen. "You can't take a slave north unless you post a bond for him."

"But I don't have any papers," Ellen protested.

"Sorry then, but we can't be responsible. If a slave goes north and escapes, the railroad has to pay the owner." The train whistle sounded. "Move aside," the ticket agent said impatiently. "Let the next person get a ticket. The train's about to leave."

It was a desperate moment. As he stood there under the leaden winter sky, William's courage faltered. "My master's sick," he said. "We've come almost 1,000 miles to see a doctor in Philadelphia. If he doesn't get treatment soon, he will die." He looked anxiously at Ellen. The agent stared at her too. She certainly looked sick. The agent chewed on his cigar and frowned.

"That's right," said a man William recognized as having been on the train with them. "I know that young gentleman. He's a planter from Georgia. His slave has been with him all the way." A few other people agreed.

The agent hesitated. Again the whistle sounded. Then he growled, "All right. All right." He handed Ellen a pair of tickets and her change.

As the attentive "slave" guided his sick "master" to the train, tears of joy were hidden behind the green glasses of the "master." But the "slave" wore the broadest of grins. William and Ellen boarded the train, knowing full well they had done what they had longed to do — escape.